W9-BZM-634

Live Love Laugh

Jean Davidson's
HARLEY-DAVIDSON
Family Album

100 Years of the World's
Greatest Motorcycle in Rare Photos

By Jean Davidson

Forewords by Sarah Harley and Arthur Harley Davidson

Voyageur Press

Photo on jacket spine by Ken Webb and Norm Zierk.

On the frontispiece: *My grandfather, Walter Davidson, with my father in the sidecar. My father, Gordon, with me in the sidecar. Here I am in 2001 just before the publication of my first book,* Growing Up Harley-Davidson.

On the title pages: *Jean Davidson, 2002. (Photograph by William Netzel) Inset on the title page: Walter Davidson, 1916*

On these pages: *The Butte, Montana, Motorcycle Club shows off its Harley-Davidsons and other early motorcycles in 1914.*

Edited by Michael Dregni
Designed by Maria Friedrich
Printed in China

03 04 05 06 07   5 4 3 2 1

Library of Congress Cataloging-in-Publication Data
Davidson, Jean, 1937-
   Jean Davidson's Harley-Davidson family album : 100 years of the world's greatest motorcycle in rare photos / by Jean Davidson ; forewords by Sarah Harley and Arthur Harley Davidson.
       p. cm.
   Includes index.
    ISBN 0-89658-629-4 (hardcover)
   1. Davidson family—Photograph collections. 2. Harley family—Photograph collections. 3. Motorcycles—United States—Biography. 4. Harley-Davidson Incorporated—History. 5. Harley-Davidson motorcycle—History. I. Title: Harley-Davidson family album. II. Title.
   TL140.D34 D38 2003
   629.227'5'0973022—dc21

                                                    2002151809

Distributed in Canada by Raincoast Books, 9050 Shaughnessy Street, Vancouver, B.C. V6P 6E5

Published by Voyageur Press, Inc.
123 North Second Street, P.O. Box 338
Stillwater, MN 55082 U.S.A.
651-430-2210, fax 651-430-2211
books@voyageurpress.com
www.voyageurpress.com

Educators, fundraisers, premium and gift buyers, publicists, and marketing managers: Looking for creative products and new sales ideas? Voyageur Press books are available at special discounts when purchased in quantities, and special editions can be created to your specifications. For details contact the marketing department at 800-888-9653.

Dedication

I would like to dedicate this book to my five children—Lori Jean, Jon Johnston, William McLay, Susan Elizabeth, and Peter John—who are the great-grandchildren of Walter Davidson. They encouraged me to follow my dream of listening to the riders by finding more personal family stories and priceless photos to share with Harley-Davidson enthusiasts all over the world.

It is also dedicated to all the wonderful people who have shared their stories and photos.

I thank you all.

Acknowledgments

I am especially thankful to Mary Harley Stocking and Sarah Harley-O'Hearn. They are two of the granddaughters of William Sylvester Harley, and have taken their time to bring precious personal family photos and stories of the Harley families to help make this book complete.

My thanks as well to Katherine Davidson, Jerry Hatfield, Herbert Wagner, Robert Jameson, and Elizabeth Moyle for all of their invaluable help in creating this collection.

Archie Rife's Winning Three-Speed

Contents

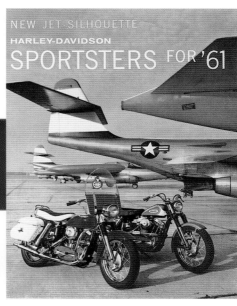

Forewords

As I ride my own Harley-Davidson motorcycle down the open road, I still find it hard to believe that it was more than 100 years ago that my grandfather, William Sylvester Harley, and the Davidson brothers took a far-fetched idea and created a legend. That legend is still alive and thriving today.

Through the years, the Harley and Davidson families have been close friends, sharing our lives and passing down through the generations stories about the founders and their legacy, the Harley-Davidson motorcycle. Jean Davidson has collected together many of these stories and pictures from our family albums far and wide, offering a vision of the founders as they were, doing what they enjoyed in life, and following their story through today. I hope that all riders and non-riders enjoy the family history and stories that Jean has worked so hard to assemble for you.

Ride safe—and enjoy this book!

Sarah Ann Harley-O'Hearn

Sarah Harley-O'Hearn on her 95th Anniversary Heritage Springer Softail with her husband Bruce O'Hearn. (Sarah Harley-O'Hearn collection)

Because so many riders and readers enjoyed our first book, *Growing Up Harley-Davidson*, Jean asked me to collaborate with her again and go further into the heart of the Harley-Davidson mystique. This family photo album is the result.

I hope you will enjoy this one as much as our first book—we certainly had fun collecting the memories and photos to put it all together.

Arthur Harley Davidson

Introduction

While traveling the country visiting Harley-Davidson dealers, making appearances at motorcycle rallies, and speaking at other engagements with my first book, *Growing Up Harley-Davidson,* I found that Harley-Davidson riders feel a close family bond with the company's founding fathers and their families. They always ask, "What more do you know? We want to see and hear more about the personal side of the founders—Walter Davidson, his brothers William and Arthur, and their best friend and partner William Harley." These men, their children, and the people who worked for them dedicated their lives to making the Harley-Davidson motorcycle a most treasured family possession. It's thus little wonder that this strong connection has continued through the years. Harley-Davidson—the founders, the company, the motorcycles, the riders— are, after all, one large family.

So here we go! Enjoy the ride and the read with a look at more personal stories and never-before-seen photos of the founders of the Harley-Davidson Motor Company, their families, and the workers who dedicated their lives to making the Harley-Davidson motorcycle beloved all over the world.

Everywhere I go, people come up and share their treasured stories about the early years working with my grandfather, Walter, my father, Gordon, and the other founders and their children down at the factory. What comes through is how close the three Davidson brothers were with their best friend and partner Bill Harley, and how these families worked and played together, dedicating their lives to following their dream of developing the highest-quality motorcycle that is now loved the world over. I have included many of these stories and photos as well.

Jean Davidson

Jean Davidson: "Here we are, from left: Sarah Harley-O'Hearn, myself, and Mary Harley Stocking sorting through photographs for this book."

Davidson Clan Family Tree

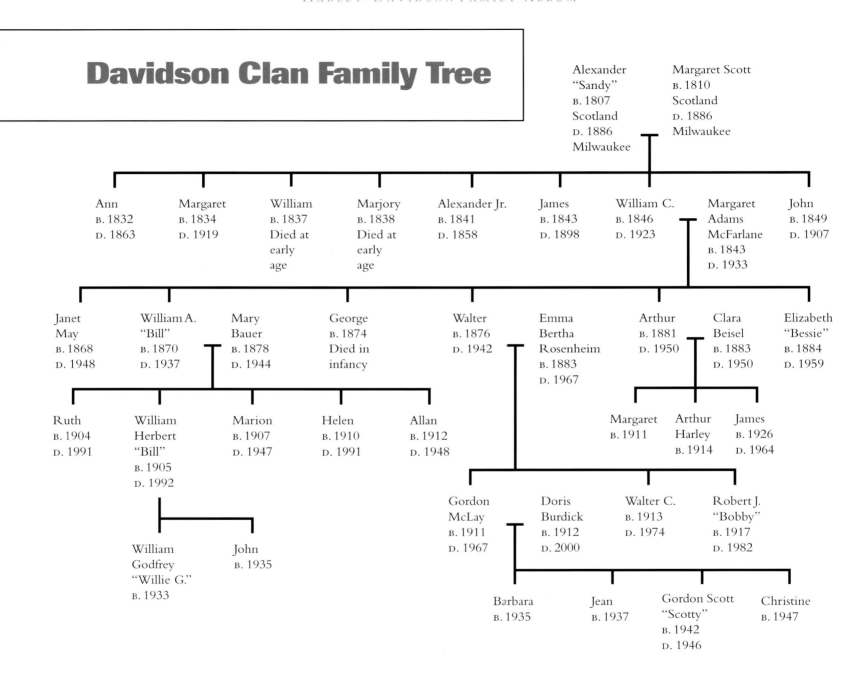

Alexander "Sandy"
B. 1807
Scotland
D. 1886
Milwaukee

Margaret Scott
B. 1810
Scotland
D. 1886
Milwaukee

Ann
B. 1832
D. 1863

Margaret
B. 1834
D. 1919

William
B. 1837
Died at
early
age

Marjory
B. 1838
Died at
early
age

Alexander Jr.
B. 1841
D. 1858

James
B. 1843
D. 1898

William C.
B. 1846
D. 1923

Margaret
Adams
McFarlane
B. 1843
D. 1933

John
B. 1849
D. 1907

Janet
May
B. 1868
D. 1948

William A.
"Bill"
B. 1870
D. 1937

Mary
Bauer
B. 1878
D. 1944

George
B. 1874
Died in
infancy

Walter
B. 1876
D. 1942

Emma
Bertha
Rosenheim
B. 1883
D. 1967

Arthur
B. 1881
D. 1950

Clara
Beisel
B. 1883
D. 1950

Elizabeth
"Bessie"
B. 1884
D. 1959

Ruth
B. 1904
D. 1991

William
Herbert
"Bill"
B. 1905
D. 1992

Marion
B. 1907
D. 1947

Helen
B. 1910
D. 1991

Allan
B. 1912
D. 1948

Margaret
B. 1911

Arthur
Harley
B. 1914

James
B. 1926
D. 1964

William
Godfrey
"Willie G."
B. 1933

John
B. 1935

Gordon
McLay
B. 1911
D. 1967

Doris
Burdick
B. 1912
D. 2000

Walter C.
B. 1913
D. 1974

Robert J.
"Bobby"
B. 1917
D. 1982

Barbara
B. 1935

Jean
B. 1937

Gordon Scott
"Scotty"
B. 1942
D. 1946

Christine
B. 1947

Harley Clan Family Tree

William
B. ?
England
D. ?

M. Smith
B. ?
England
D. ?

| Katherine "Katie" B. 1868 D. 1943 | Joseph B. 1870 D. 1950 | Mary "May" B. 1873 D. 1876 | Anastasia "Hannah" B. 1874 D. 1876 | Susan B. 1875 D. 1877 | William Sylvester B. 1880 D. 1943 | Anna Jachtuber B. 1882 D. 1954 | Charles B. 1882 D. 1882 |

Rosemary
Muth
B. 1912
D. 1992

William
James
B. 1912
D. 1971

Ann
Mary
B. 1914
D. 1975

John
Edward
B. 1915
D. 1976

Kathryn May
Womeldorf
B. 1920
D. 1994

| William B. 1938 | Mary B. 1940 | Robert B. 1945 | Roseanne B. 1948 | John Edward Jr. B. 1945 | James P. B. 1948 | Sarah Ann B. 1956 |

Note: These family trees only show Harley and Davidson family members mentioned in this book.

Immigrants to the New World

The Harley and the Davidson families were immigrants to the United States, arriving in the late 1800s with the promise of starting a new life in the frontier state of Wisconsin.

Sarah Harley: "My great-grandparents, William Harley and Mary Smith, immigrated to the United States from Littleport, England. My grandfather, William Sylvester Harley, was born in America in 1880. Here is his wife, Anna, standing, and son, John, on the running board, during an outing in circa 1918." (Sarah Harley-O'Hearn collection)

Jean Davidson: "My great-great-grandfather, Alexander 'Sandy' Davidson, and his wife, Margaret Scott, set sail with their six children from Scotland to America in 1858. They came first to Winneconne, Wisconsin, where Margaret's relatives had settled. After a time, Sandy found work as a carpenter with the Chicago, Milwaukee & St. Paul Railroad, which required him to pack up his family and move to Milwaukee."

Left: *Jean Davidson: "Here are my great-grand-parents and other relatives. Seated from left: William C. and his wife, Margaret McFarlane Davidson, the parents of the founders; and James McLay, the Honey Uncle. Standing behind them are Janet May, the oldest daughter, who painted the letters on the shed door and the logos on the first motorcycles, and Elisabeth, who kept the books for the young company in the early years."*

Above: *Emblem of the Davidson clan and tartan from the family's homeland, Scotland.*

Two Boys With a Dream

Arthur Davidson and William Harley were childhood chums and next-door neighbors. Smitten by the blossoming age of technology and dreaming of creating new motorized inventions, they began building their "motor-bicycle" in the basement carpentry workshop of Arthur's father, William C. Davidson.

Jean Davidson: "Arthur, kneeling, was friends with Ole Evinrude, standing in the middle. In 1902, they started their own pattern-making company; here they pose with a pattern and their two employees. When Arthur and Bill crafted a primitive carburetor for their motorcycle engine using a tomato-soup can as the throttle body, they had problems getting the fuel flow right. It was Ole who offered his help in perfecting the first Harley-Davidson carburetor."

Sarah Harley: "William Harley, right, got early engineering experience while working here at Milwaukee's Meiselbach Bicycle factory in 1901. Based on his knowledge of bicycle frames, he knew that the standard 'diamond-shaped' bicycle frame that most early motorcycles used was too flimsy to carry a motor. He eventually created a 'loop' frame that worked so well that Harley-Davidson continued to use the design for decades."

Arthur Davidson

Arthur Davidson was twenty when he and Bill Harley first tried their hand at building a "motor-bicycle." Arthur was an experienced pattern maker, yet when the Harley-Davidson Motor Company was legally formed on September 17, 1907, he became the secretary and general sales manager. He had a great gift of gab and loved to meet new people and travel, all of which made him the perfect salesman.

Jean Davidson: "This is Arthur, right, delivering an early Harley-Davidson to Cambridge, Wisconsin, postal carrier Pete Olson, left, for use in mail delivery. Dealer Geo. Keystin looks on."

Sarah Harley: "Here's William Harley, left, standing alongside his childhood chum and lifelong friend Arthur Davidson after a round of golf." (Sarah Harley-O'Hearn collection)

Jean Davidson: "Arthur sits on his motorcycle showing off a northern pike he caught in 1916 while on a fishing outing with his friend in the sidecar. Being the most outgoing of the brothers, Arthur was well suited to his job of selling. With his friendly personality and his gift for gab, no one was safe from his charm. If he had an idea that he thought was worth selling, watch out—he was unstoppable." (Herbert Wagner collection)

William Sylvester Harley

William Harley was twenty-one when he and Arthur Davidson began building their "motor-bicycle." After the company was founded, Bill loved to spend hours at his drafting table, working on engineering the motorcycles. He took on the role of chief engineer and treasurer.

Sarah Harley: "William Harley at the summit of Pikes Peak in Colorado in his sidecar rig. He and his friend are parked in front of the Pikes Peak Auto Highway Depot, which was the highest building in the United States at the time." (Sarah Harley-O'Hearn collection)

William A. Davidson

The eldest brother, Bill Davidson, felt most at home on the shop floor rubbing elbows with the other machinists and working the tools. He left behind his job as a railroad toolroom foreman to become works manager for the new Harley-Davidson Motor Company.

Sarah Harley: "Here they are using their motorcycles the way they intended: to go fishing. William Davidson stands with a northern pike caught in 1924 in Pine Lake in Hartland, Wisconsin. My grandfather, William Harley, sits on the motorcycle." (Sarah Harley-O'Hearn collection)

Walter Davidson

Walter Davidson was Arthur's elder brother and a skilled mechanic and machinist. He worked in Parsons, Kansas, for the Missouri, Kansas & Texas Railroad. When Walter came home for William Davidson's wedding, Bill Harley and Arthur invited him for a ride on their new machine. Little did Walter know he first had to assemble it. Walter was intrigued by the business end of things and was named company president.

"When my grandfather Walter was thirteen years old, he became very interested in electricity. Working in his parents' basement, he practiced electro-plating, and his mom had to watch out to save everything in their home from having its finish changed to something else. He loved to copper-, nickel-, and silver-plate anything in the house that he could. His next adventure turned out to be storage-battery manufacture. After he made one successfully, he was fascinated by the first electric streetcar. He was right on the cutting edge of electrical innovation. He took a job in Milwaukee as an electrical contractor and worked for a few years wiring buildings in Milwaukee—and this was on top of being a mechanic by trade. He went up to work at a railroad shop in Minneapolis for a short time and then went to Parsons, Kansas, where the famous Missouri, Kansas & Texas Railway Company was called the 'Katy Road.'"

—Jean Davidson

Jean Davidson: "My grandfather, Walter, was a self-taught businessman and spent his spare time reading and studying. He learned how to weld and other skills, and then taught his employees."

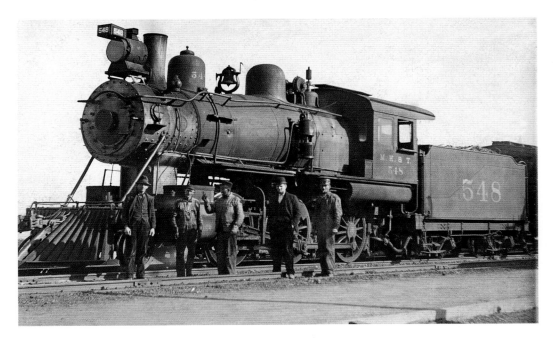

"Walter bought his first bicycle in 1893 when he was seventeen years old. It was a second-hand Remington bought at auction for $35. He was always taking the bike apart and putting it together again in the family kitchen because he wanted it to be in perfect shape at all times. He participated in bicycle road races, and trained by riding from Madison to Milwaukee in ten hours. That is 80 miles from the state capital to his home!"

—Jean Davidson

Top left: *Jean Davidson: "This is a locomotive on the famous Katy Road in Parsons, Kansas, where my grandfather worked from 1901 to 1903. That's Walter second from right." (Maynard Harding collection)*

Bottom left: *Jean Davidson: "When a job was well done at the plant, my grandfather, Walter Davidson, would climb up on the factory rooftop and raise a flag that could be seen less than a mile away by his buddy Fritz Gettleman, right, who ran Milwaukee's famous Gettleman brewery—it's now the Miller brewery. Fritz would then bring a barrel of beer up to the factory for all of the employees to celebrate."*

The Motorcycle Born in a Shed

Great-Grandmother Margaret Davidson was famed for keeping a neat house, and she couldn't stand the boys building their "motor-bicycle" in her basement, tracking dirt and grease in and out all the time. One day, she had enough and kicked the boys and their invention out of the basement. The Davidson's father, William C., felt sorry for them and built a backyard shed to serve as their workshop. Now the young inventors could go out into their own shed and make all the noise they needed.

Jean Davidson: "Here's the famous shed where the first Harley-Davidson motorcycle was built. Old-time dealer Hap Jameson remembered the old shed was to be burned down by the company sometime in the 1950s. He raised hell with President Bill Davidson and saved it! The shed survived for many years in the shadow of the new works. It was finally torn down by mistake by a maintenance worker who was told to clean up the grounds."

Harley-Davidson or Davidson-Harley?

Why the name Harley-Davidson? Why not Davidson-Harley? Some family members say since there was only one Harley, the founders thought his name should be first out of politeness. Another story goes that as Bill Harley was one year older than Arthur, his name went first. Yet another story states that since Harley drew the plans, he was more important in the motorcycle's creation. I think they were just two friends with a dream and no idea their invention would become a worldwide icon. They did not care whose name came first. "Harley-Davidson" simply flowed off of the tongue better than "Davidson-Harley."

Jean Davidson: "Janet Davidson, the oldest sister in the family, had an artistic flair. When her father built the shed, she could not resist adding her touch. Finding a can of paint, she hand-painted the letters on the door: HARLEY DAVIDSON MOTOR CO. When the first motorcycles rolled out the door, Janet was out in the shed hand-painting the logo on the tanks and painting red pinstriping on each tank and fender."

The Silent Gray Fellows

Because William Harley was a quiet, reserved man whose hair had turned silvery gray at an early age, he was affectionately known as the "Silent Gray Fellow" by the other founders. And because Bill Harley was the company's respected chief engineer, the Davidson brothers nicknamed Harley's latest motorcycle in his honor.

Mary Harley: "The original Silent Gray Fellow, my grandfather, William Sylvester Harley." (Mary Harley Stocking collection)

Left: *Two men pose on a Silent Gray Fellow in the 1910s.*

Above: *William S. Harley's namesake, the Silent Gray Fellow motorcycle, from a Harley-Davidson advertising slide for 1914.*

The First Harley-Davidson

The first Harley-Davidson from 1903 was sold to Henry Meyer, who rode it 6,000 miles and then sold it to George Lyon, who put 15,000 more miles on it. The next three owners were Dr. Webster, Louis Fluke, and Steve J. Sparough. Between the three of them, another 62,000 miles of dependable travel was put on the bike. Not one of these owners ever had to replace the bearings.

Steve J. Sparough's 1912 letter chronicling the early owners of the first Harley-Davidson.

Jean Davidson: "This was the first Harley-Davidson as it was later pictured in The Harley-Davidson Dealer *in 1912. I had dinner with the son of Henry Meyer in the fall of 2001, and he remembered his dad talking about what fun he had riding around on this first Harley-Davidson and showing it off all over Milwaukee. It was a true marvel at the time, and everyone wanted a look at it."*

The Thomas B. Jeffery Company
Of Illinois.

Chicago, Ill., April 15th, 1912.

Harley-Davidson Motor Co.,
Mr. C. H. Lang, Ill. Distributor,
Chicago, Illinois.

Dear Sir:-

When I bought my Harley-Davidson Motorcycle, which I still have in daily use, it had already run 51,000 miles.

According to my information it is the first Harley-Davidson that was ever built. It was made in 1903 and sold in 1904 to Mr. Mayer of Milwaukee who rode it 6,000 miles. Geo. V. Lyon of Chicago rode it 15,000 miles. Dr. Webster of Rush Medical College of Chicago rode it 18,000 miles. Louis Fluke rode it 12,000 miles.

I bought this machine from Louis Fluke in 1907 and have ridden it to date 32,000 miles, which makes a total of 83,000 miles. It is in perfect condition and still has the same main bearings.

It has a 3 1-4 H.P. motor and 26.94 cubic inches piston displacement, the largest sized motor used in motorcycles at that time.

I am repairman for the Thomas B. Jeffery Company the Chicago branch where the Rambler automobiles are sold and kept in repair. I make trips with my machine to repair cars, if they get into trouble out in the country.

I also use it daily to and from work, besides using it during business hours. It has given me entire satisfaction as it is always on the job and always makes good when called upon for service.

The new Harley-Davidson now has wonderful improvements over my old model, but I would not like to sell it, because it has stood by me rain or shine. It is now nine years in service and will make good for many more years.

Yours very truly,

Steve J Sparough

The Honey Uncle Saves the Day

In the early days, the founders did not have a company bank account; they used an old canning jar in the pantry as their "bank." Sadly, in 1904, a household maid in need of money raided the jar, and all Harley-Davidson's earnings were gone. Just when things seemed hopeless, help arrived from a surprising source. The Davidson boys had a hermit uncle named James McLay who came to their rescue. Upon hearing of the boys' plight, he loaned them every penny of his life savings.

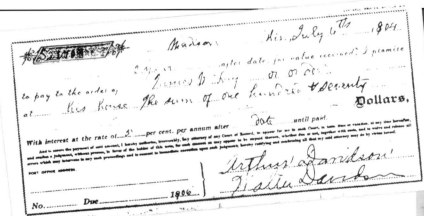

Above: *The receipt given to the Honey Uncle on July 6, 1904.*

Right: *Jean Davidson: "Hermit uncle James MacLay, standing, with his brother Moses visited the Davidson family in Milwaukee in 1904 and was intrigued by the motorcycle dreams of young Arthur, Walter, and Bill Harley. Known affectionately as the Honey Uncle, he was paid back tenfold and was always honored by the founders.*

Simple and Sensible Motorcycles

The first Harley-Davidson motorcycles were not flashy machines. Rather than being racers or speedsters, they became famous for being reliable motorcycles that would run forever. This was just the way the boys wanted them. Their engineering sense and the respect the motorcycles earned fit well with the boys' English and Scottish heritage, which stood strong for the simple, practical, and sensible.

"In the early years, the four founders did everything in their 'factory'. They made the motorcycles, they tested them, they crated them, and they sold them."
—Jean Davidson

A 1912 advertisement for the 5-35 single.

Jean Davidson: "Harley-Davidson built its reputation first on its simple and reliable single-cylinder machines, such as this 1912 single."

Jean Davidson: "The singles also won their share of races. Here's Charles F. Barrett on his single-cylinder that won the Utica, New York, Auto Club hillclimb in 1915, beating out the fastest car."

Gone Fishing

Three of the four founders were enamored with fishing. Part of the impetus for building their first motorcycle was to provide a quicker way rather than walking to get to their favorite fishing hole. Through the years, many advertisements and photos continued to promote the combined joys of fishing trips and Harley-Davidson motorcycles.

"Harley-Davidson's president, Walter Davidson, was the only one of the founders that didn't love to hunt or fish. The other three were especially crazy for fishing, and Walter would often go along on these trips but not fish. As William S. Harley remembered, Walter had so much energy that when they went fishing, Walter rowed the boat: 'Walter's surplus energy is fine stuff around the factory,' Bill Harley once said, 'but when we go fishing, he has to row the boat. The only way we can use it is to have him furnish the motive power. Walter Davidson was the epitome of a man with motive power.'"

—Jean Davidson

Above: *Jean Davidson: "Even my grandmother Emma, far right, had to go fishing. Here she's holding a northern pike in horror—and wearing a snazzy fur-trimmed coat at the same time!"*

Right: *Sarah Harley: "The founders—except for Walter Davidson—simply loved fishing. Here they are with some buddies with a good catch. William Davidson is at far left. Arthur is fourth from left. William Harley holds his pipe. Walter is third from right." (Sarah Harley-O'Hearn collection)*

The Debut of the V-Twin

Harley-Davidson's laurels have long rested on its famous V-twins, but it was not until 1909—six years after the company was founded—that the firm released its first V-twin-engined motorcycle. To add to the irony, that 1909 V-twin did not return for the 1910 model year. It was not until 1911 that the V-twin was back to stay.

1915 Harley-Davidson

11 real horsepower guaranteed
3-speed sliding gear transmission
Automatic mechanical oil pump
Starter on all models
66 refinements
Lower prices

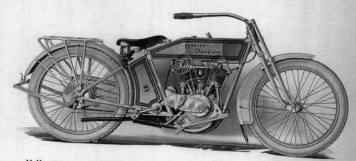

New Harley-Davidson
11 Horsepower Guaranteed

11 Horsepower, Twin Model 11-E (shown above) F. O. B. Milwaukee, ... $240
11 Horsepower, Close-Coupled Stripped Stock Model 11-K (not illustrated) F. O. B. Milwaukee, $250

The 1915 motor is a new motor throughout. It embodies altogether 29 changes and refinements over the 1914 motor. With no greater piston displacement than the 1914 twin, the Harley-Davidson engineers have increased the power output 31 per cent at 2,500 revolutions per minute and 47 per cent at 3,000 revolutions per minute.

The same refinements which made this increased power and speed possible are responsible for a marked decrease in both gasoline and oil consumption and higher all-around efficiency. The new motor shows absolutely no vibration on the road. For flexibility it is a marvel—the snappiest, liveliest power plant ever put into a motorcycle.

The Harley-Davidson automatic mechanical oil pump is partly responsible for the increased speed and power of the new motor, but new cylinders, faster valve mechanism, larger inlet gas ports, a new type of inlet valves with 45° seats, larger than before, together with a larger intake manifold and carburetor, and heavier fly wheels, are some of the important changes noticeable.

The precise lubrication of the new motor, perfect combustion of gas, perfect scavenging of burnt gases, and the elimination of practically all motor vibration, will materially increase the life of the Harley-Davidson motor.

The 1915 Harley-Davidson is the First Motorcycle

Left: *The cover of a 1915 advertising flyer for the V-twin.*

Above: *Harley-Davidson guaranteed 11 horsepower from its 1915 V-twin.*

Facing page: *Jean Davidson: "This beautiful painting of a rider and his V-twin appeared in a 1913 issue of* The Harley-Davidson Dealer *magazine and was used on 1913 advertising posters."*

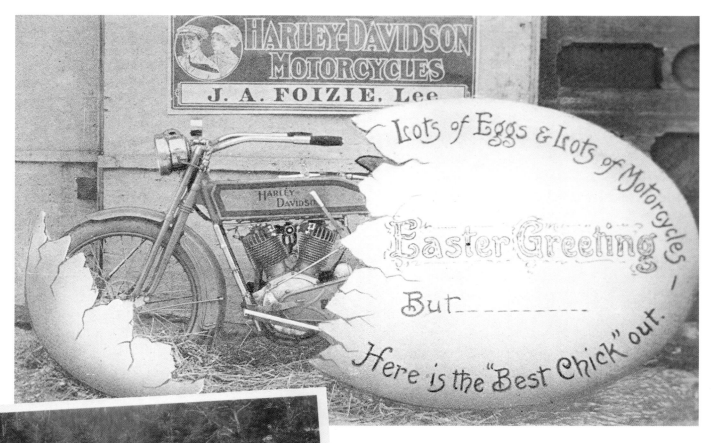

Above: *Humorous dealer postcard for the new 1914 Harley-Davidson V-twin.*

Left: *Harley-Davidson riders on an outing in 1921.*

Jean Davidson: "The V-twin proved to be an ideal motorcycle for hauling a sidecar, which was a popular setup in those days as it provided inexpensive transportation for a young family. Here's a group of Harley-Davidson fans preparing for a ride." (Robert Jameson collection)

Left: *Jean Davidson: "Here is Hap Jameson with a young lass, photographed for an ad or sales catalog. Hap was racing motorcycles in 1910 when Arthur Davidson met him and asked him to come to Milwaukee and work for the company. Hap became the first instructor at the factory service school. He later became a dealer in Evanston, Illinois." (Robert Jameson collection)*

Above: *Jean Davidson: "Here's the repair shop at Hap Mundy's Harley-Davidson dealership. Quite a crowded place!"*

Right: *Jean Davidson: "Harley-Davidson also tried to build what it called an 'aristocratic' machine, the opposed-twin Sport. Sadly, it was a dismal failure."*

Right: *A Harley-Davidson sidecar outfit navigates a snowy road.*

Facing page, left: *Jean Davidson: "Here are Walter Davidson, left, and William Harley at a 1920s motorcycle rally."*

Facing page, right: *Sarah Harley: "Here's William S. Harley in a sidecar near Colorado Springs, Colorado, during a trip out west in the 1920s." (Sarah Harley-O'Hearn collection)*

Harley-Davidson 1931 advertisement.

Left: *Jean Davidson: "These were the pleasures of motorcycling Harley-Davidson style in the 1920s and 1930s."*

Above and right: *Harley-Davidson 1930 sales catalogs.*

To Race or Not to Race?

Initially, the founders of Harley-Davidson would have nothing to do with racing. They built their first motorcycle to carry them to the fishing hole, and the early machines retained this practical, reliable, no-nonsense personality. Arthur in particular was staunchly against racing and waged a campaign in the pages of *The Harley-Davidson Dealer* in 1912 warning all dealers against it. Only in 1913 did Harley-Davidson change its corporate mind on racing and actively challenge Indian and other motorcycle makers on the racetrack. Indian had been racing in Milwaukee right under Harley-Davidson's nose, and it simply became too much to take. When Harley-Davidson decided to go racing, the company made the decision to race to win. And win it did.

Both ads: *Jean Davidson: "When Harley-Davidson finally decided to go racing, it went all out. The Harley-Davidson Dealer was full of articles and photos bragging about the factory's victories."*

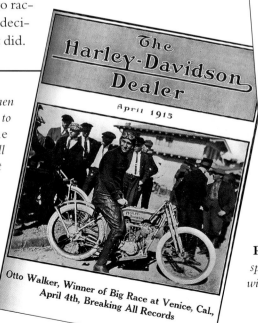

April 1915

Otto Walker, Winner of Big Race at Venice, Cal., April 4th, Breaking All Records

A New World's Record

Ray Watkins and Ben Torres Ride 346 Miles in 7 hours on a dirt track with an 8 H.P. Harley-Davidson

AT San Jose, Cal., December 8th, the regular stock eight horse power Harley-Davidson established a new world's record by covering 346 miles in seven hours.

The winning Harley-Davidson team finished 17 miles ahead of their nearest competitor and more than 12 miles ahead of the former world's record, although it was made on a board track. In addition to winning the first prize the Harley-Davidson also made the fastest mile in the contest.

During the whole run not a single repair, replacement or even adjustment was made to the Harley-Davidson and not a stop of any nature whatsoever was made except for change of riders and to take on gasoline and oil.

RAY WATKINS   BEN TORRES

As manufacturers we do not support racing and do not build racing machines. This new record came as a complete surprise to us. The contest was conducted entirely without our knowledge and the first we heard of it was a newspaper clipping sent in to the factory.

We have repeatedly asserted that the eight horse power Harley-Davidson was the fastest stock machine made, barring none. This has been proved time and again in contests where private owners competed with their own machines. This San Jose victory furnishes more actual proof that the Harley-Davidson will stand up under the most trying conditions possible and at a maintained high speed. The Harley-Davidson averaged 49.43 miles per hour for the entire 7 hours, including all stops for gas and oil.

The San Jose contest was conducted under F. A. M. sanction.

Harley-Davidson Motor Company
Producers of High-Grade Motorcycles for Eleven Years

Right: *Jean Davidson: "Ever since I was a child, motorcycle racing had a special place in my heart. All the racers I met were lean, strong, graceful, and wiry. I thought they were brave and had excellent coordination and balance."*

From Wooden Shed to Brick Factory

With funding from the Honey Uncle and new orders coming in, the founders built in 1906 their first true factory on what was then called Chestnut Street but was soon renamed Juneau Avenue. The new factory measured twenty-eight by eighty feet. Being new in the building business, no one thought to survey the property lines. One day an agent for the railroad came and told them their new building was on railroad property. The founders and their employees solved the problem in a logical way: Together, they picked up the wood building, moved it a foot and a half off the railroad land, and went back to work.

Above: *Jean Davidson: "Here's a photo of the famous shed in 1903 with Janet Davidson's 'logo' hand-painted on the front door."*

Right: *Jean Davidson: "Here's the first factory building, which was built a block from the original shed. It was at the corner of 38th and Chestnut Avenue."*

"A longtime worker named Kenneth Flanum at the Harley-Davidson Capitol Drive Plant remembered his first day on the job in 1964 as a drillpress operator. My father, Gordon Davidson, came up to him and said, 'Let me introduce myself to you as you are new on the job here.' Gordon would go to work on Saturdays and stay down on the shop floor. He dressed in jeans and a tee-shirt. He knew everyone by name and shared stories with all, asking about people's families. It was obvious to all of the shop workers, as Flanum stated, that Gordon truly loved his company. He was so down to earth and easy to talk with."

—Jean Davidson

This Immense Plant is Devoted Exclusively to the Manufacture of Harley-Davidson Motorcycles

Jean Davidson: "By 1920, the now-famous Harley-Davidson factory on West Juneau Avenue had grown many times over and was one of the largest and most important businesses in Milwaukee. Juneau Avenue was named in honor of Solomon Juneau, a French Canadian fur trader who became Milwaukee's first mayor."

Jean Davidson: "The employees of the Harley-Davidson company in 1907 pose with one of the single-cylinder engines in front of the 2,380-square-foot wooden factory building. That's President Walter Davidson kneeling on the far right. Arthur is kneeling third from right. William, with his mustache, is standing second from right."

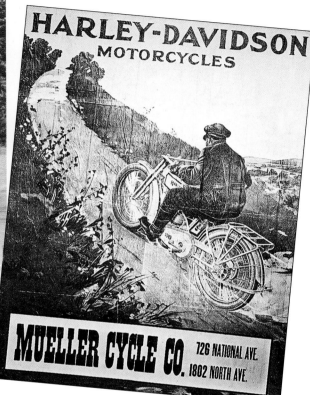

Sarah Harley: "This was the garage at the factory where the family parked their cars or motorcycles when they arrived at work. When they were ready to go home at the end of the day, their machines were always freshly washed and waiting for them. Here's William S. Harley on his way home after a day of work." (Robert Jameson collection)

A 1915 Harley-Davidson poster.

"Don Poznanski remembered starting out in 1965 at Harley-Davidson on the assembly line on the third floor at Juneau Avenue. He didn't have much money and was building his own motorcycle from scratch. Gordon would always come down on the floor and ask him how it was going. One day, Poznanski told him he needed a certain model seat to fit his bike; he knew the policy that if something was damaged he could buy it for less, but none of the seats were damaged. Gordon went over, picked up the seat, took out his pocket knife and made a few scratches on the bottom of the seat. He handed the seat to Kenneth and said, 'Here, you can have this damaged one.'"

—Jean Davidson

Testing Motorcycles

In the early years, each new motorcycle was tested out on the road as soon as it rolled off the assembly line to make certain everything was in perfect order.

Jean Davidson: "Here are the employees at the famous Maggini & Perkins Harley-Davidson dealership in San Francisco standing in front of the shop with a lineup of motorcycles still in their factory shipping crates."

Right: *Jean Davidson: "A completed machine is put through its paces climbing the hill on Chestnut Street to the side of the factory. At times, Walter Davidson used to test the new machines personally to doublecheck the quality level. He rode them alongside the railroad tracks behind the factory—and the old-time workers used to tell how he even raced trains for fun when an old steam locomotive happened to come by." (Robert Jameson collection)*

Left: *Jean Davidson: "Here are a group of factory workers lined up with several new Harley-Davidsons ready to go out on a test ride."*

Left: *Jean Davidson: "Here was the next generation of Harley and Davidson boys grouped together for a picture on their normal modes of transportation around Milwaukee. From left: Walter C., Gordon, and Allan Davidson, and Bill Harley."*

Another Milwaukee Industry Becomes a World-Leader

HARLEY-Davidson excellence has received world recognition. The superb performance of this highly developed motorcycle has won for it a place in the lead of all other motorcycles.

HARLEY-DAVIDSON MOTORCYCLES

are sold in 67 countries. There are now more Harley-Davidsons in use in this country than any other make.

Milwaukee is the home of the largest producer of motorcycles and sidecars in the world. The Harley-Davidson Motorcycle is carrying information of Milwaukee's greatness, and is demonstrating the real worth of Milwaukee's products, to the far corners of the earth.

Harley-
Davidson
Motor
Company

MILWAUKEE

The Founders and Their Families

Perhaps amazingly, the founders all remained good friends through the years. They worked together and often played and vacationed together. The founders all lived close to the factory so they could be near work. And they worked so hard that Walter's wife, Emma, used to say she was lucky if Walter was home by 8 P.M. on Christmas Eve. Through the years, the founders' families also became friends, growing up alongside each other with the children running in and out of each other's homes.

Facing page: *Jean Davidson: "Here are the four founders in the 1920s standing in front of the factory. From left: William A., Walter, Arthur, and William S. Harley. Each of the founders took positions in the company that perfectly fit their personalities. It's amazing how well they complemented each other in creating a company."*

Jean Davidson: "From left, here is Bill Harley's wife, Ann; Walter's wife, Emma; William A.'s wife, Mary; and Arthur's wife, Clara."

Sarah Harley: "The four company founders were also founding members of the Milwaukee Athletic Club. Here they are dressed up in funny outfits at the MAC on October 25, 1913. Walter is at left. Arthur is fourth from left. William is third from right William Harley is at far right."

Left: *Jean Davidson: "Walter married a German bar-owner's daughter named Emma—it was a true Cinderella story come to life! Emma was a feisty lady, full of personality with many hobbies and interests. Here they are on a business trip to Europe in the early 1930s, traveling in style." (Katherine Davidson collection)*

Above: *Jean Davidson: "When one of the founder's wives needed to be brought somewhere or simply wanted to go for a ride, the factory sent out a sidecar outfit with an employee who acted as a sort of chauffeur to take them wherever they needed to go. Here is Arthur Davidson's wife, Clara, out for a ride with her first daughter, Margaret, in about 1914."*

Jean Davidson: "Here's my dad, Gordon, with his maternal grandfather, Adolph Rosenheim, who ran a bar just down the street from the Harley-Davidson factory."

Jean Davidson: "Here's my dad, Gordon, at left, with his younger brother Walter sticking his tongue out at him in about 1916." (Katherine Davidson collection)

Jean Davidson: "Walter loved his children and was fond of fun and games. Here he is at Pewaukee Lake with his kids and the other founders' children playing games by the water."

Jean Davidson: "My grandfather, Walter, had two Scottish kilts brought over from Scotland for his children to wear whenever there was a parade or celebration. That's Gordon on the left with Walter. Grandfather called in a photographer to take their picture, which started a family tradition in which each generation had its picture taken in these kilts in remembrance of their heritage. When I was a young girl, my picture was taken with my sister in these same kilts, and when I had children, the tradition continued." (Katherine Davidson collection)

Left: *Jean Davidson: "Here are some of the founders' children enjoying the summer at Lakeside Resort at Pewaukee Lake, thirty miles from Milwaukee, in about 1920. From front to back: Bobbie Davidson, Walter C., Gordon, and Ann Harley."* *(Katherine Davidson collection)*

Above: *Jean Davidson: "Katherine Drmolka was hired as a nanny when she was just fourteen years old and eventually stayed her whole life with Walter Davidson's family. First, she raised Gordon, left, and Walter C. Then she took care of their mother, Emma, until she died. The boys thought of Katherine as their second mother and, in turn, took care of her to her final days."* *(Katherine Davidson collection)*

Harley-Davidson Dealers

It was Arthur Davidson who first came to believe that long-term success would come only when there were dealers all over the United States selling Harley-Davidsons. He set out to accomplish this goal by building a nationwide dealer network. His motto was "Our dealers must make money, and then so will we."

Jean Davidson: "Arthur believed that dealers were gold. He felt that Harley-Davidson could only be as successful as its dealers were. These dealers became trusted friends and would be loyal outlets for Harley-Davidson products through the years. They would remain dealers in both good and bad times because of the close personal connection with Arthur. Here's Arthur visiting with dealer Reg Shanks of Brooklands Motorcycles in Victoria, British Columbia, in 1937. They're standing in front of the Victoria parliament building with a 1937 VLD 74 mounted with an English Noxal sidecar body." (Murray Anderson collection)

The Harley-Davidson Dealer

May 1912

Jean Davidson: *"Starting in 1912, the company published its first magazine,* The Harley-Davidson Dealer. *Although publication continued only through December 1915, this early magazine was packed with company information on the new models, dealer advice, and Harley-Davidson lore and legend. Here's the cover of the first issue of* The Harley-Davidson Dealer, *May 1912. This was from my grandfather Walter's own bound collection and features his signature on the first page."*

ANNOUNCEMENT

THIS is the first number of what we are going to call The Harley-Davidson Dealer. As its name signifies, The Dealer will be published for the benefit of the men who handle the Harley-Davidson motorcycle. We say benefit because this publication is the medium in which you dealers tell your troubles and your joys. It is your paper.

At the factory the manual labor of getting The Dealer ready for press will be attended to by Frank B. Rodger, a man who has had many years of newspaper experience. But understand us rightly, he is to be a helper only. The editors in reality must be you dealers. You are to be the chief contributors for this is to be your paper.

There are so many of you, so widely scattered, away around the other side of the globe now, not forgetting Porto Rico, the Hawaiian Islands and the Philippines, that it is necessary for you to have a central news bureau. The clearing house for news will of course be at the factory so send your ideas to Rodger, and let him do the clerical work necessary to get The Dealer printed, but, remember this at all times, this is your paper.

Don't be too modest in telling of your successes. Don't be reticent in telling about your troubles. Your success may help some other dealer and your troubles may bring from some other dealer his solution. Tell what you are accomplishing—how you are doing it—help the other dealer and he will help you. The Dealer is to be the disseminating news bureau, which hopes to assist in making better, bigger and more proficient dealers for the Harley-Davidson everywhere.

Your success is our success, and a factory which sells as ours does only through dealers, must have successful dealers to succeed. Remember

The Harley-Davidson Dealer is the Harley-Davidson dealer's paper

Announcement of the debut of the magazine from the first issue.

Dreaming of Dollars Doesn't Bring Them to You

Advice to dealers from the pages of The Harley-Davidson Dealer.

Jean Davidson: "By 1930, Harley-Davidson was a big business thanks to its network of dealers built up by Arthur. Here's a group of dealers and salesmen at a regional sales school and conference in Philadelphia on February 3–6, 1930. That's my father, Gordon, fourth from left in the front row." (Charlie Lecach collection)

Women Workers at Harley-Davidson

The founders did not allow married women to work at Harley-Davidson. Due to their strong sentiments concerning family values, the founders believed a married woman's duty was to her family, and there was an unwritten rule in the early years that once a female worker was married she could not stay at the factory.

Jean Davidson: "A Girls Welfare Club 'beauty contest' during a picnic at Little Cedar Lake, Wisconsin, on July 26, 1925. Founder Arthur Davidson, right, donned a women's bathing costume and joined the fun." (Elizabeth Moyle collection)

Jean Davidson: "The company sponsored a Girls Welfare Club for its young, single female workers that constantly held parties. This gathering took place on February 26, 1932, and featured several of the young women dressed in men's suits." (Elizabeth Moyle collection)

Above: *Jean Davidson: "Here's Stella Forge, the receptionist at Harley-Davidson. Stella knew everyone's business at the company because she took care of everyone's calls. Stella controlled the fate of anyone coming in the front door. If Stella did not like you, you were doomed for getting an order. You never got past her switchboard because she also controlled the doors. Most of the salesmen knew this and thus were especially nice to her."* (Elizabeth Moyle collection)

Right: *Jean Davidson: "Stella is at the controls with Elizabeth Moyle (née Durr) behind her. Liz Moyle worked at Harley-Davidson from 1923 to 1950—seventeen years in the finance department and ten years in 'Executive Row.' When she got married at age forty-four, she was let go from the company."* (Elizabeth Moyle collection)

Jean Davidson: "Bathing beauties at the Girls Welfare Club picnic with Arthur Davidson at left." (Elizabeth Moyle collection)

"There was a kind of unwritten rule that none of the Harley or Davidson women would work at the factory. I think the founders were nervous that some factory worker would marry us and try to get their hands into the family business."

—Sarah Harley

Bill Knuth: The Secret R&D Man

Bill Knuth and his brother ran the Harley-Davidson dealership on the company's home turf in Milwaukee County. But Bill was more than just a dealer, he was best friends with the founders—and served as an unofficial race team and secret, one-man Research & Development department for Harley-Davidson.

Jean Davidson: "Bill Knuth in front of the factory during the 1920s. Bill's vast experience building and tuning racing Harley-Davidsons was used by the factory in developing new models. Bill Knuth and Bill Harley used to sit around the kitchen table at one or another's home in the evening and work out motorcycle design ideas together." (Robert Jameson collection)

Jean Davidson: "Bill Knuth sponsored his own race team, the Knuth Klimbers, in the 1920s and 1930s. In 1928, the factory and Bill Knuth teamed up to build an overhead-valve 45 for hillclimb races. In 1930, Bill built a second 45 OHV hillclimber that was known as the 'Knuth Special.' Bill Knuth's work was the starting point for Bill Harley in designing the 61 OHV Knucklehead."

The Second Generation: William Herbert Davidson

Jean Davidson: "William Davidson became the U.S. national enduro champion thanks to his ride at the Jack Pine race in 1930. Here he is at about the same time on his own Flathead outside the factory."

William A. Davidson's son, William Herbert, was known by everyone as Bill Davidson. He was the eldest of the second generation of Davidsons and was the first to join the company. He eventually succeeded Walter Davidson as Harley-Davidson president.

Jean Davidson: "The sons of the founders decided they needed some adventure in their lives so they talked their parents into letting them ride Harley-Davidson motorcycles to the West Coast in 1929, stopping at dealerships along the way. Allan, Gordon, and Walter C. Davidson rode all across the western United States and into Canada and Mexico. Bill Davidson and Bill Harley joined them in Denver for the ride back to Milwaukee. Here they are, from left: Allan, Gordon, Walter C., Bill Davidson in the sidecar, and Bill J. Harley. And they never did tell their parents about the fun in Tijuana."

The Second Generation: Gordon McLay Davidson

Walter Davidson had three sons, Gordon McLay, Walter C., and Robert J. Gordon soon followed in his father's footsteps, joining Harley-Davidson in 1932 in the sales department as an accountant.

"A longtime worker named Art Winkels at the Harley-Davidson Pilgrim Plant—the old Briggs & Stratton factory—remembered a day in 1964 when Gordon came in on a Saturday when Art was working. Gordon gave Art a dime to go get himself a cup of coffee and have a break while Gordon watched his machine for him. That's the way the factory was in those days."

—Jean Davidson

Jean Davidson: "Gordon was my father. His middle name was in honor of James McLay, the Honey Uncle that saved the company back in its early days. Gordon graduated from the Wharton School of Finance at the University of Pennsylvania."

Right: *Jean Davidson: "My dad loved racing as much as I did. Here he is standing proudly next to the winning Harley-Davidson at the Springfield, Ohio, race in 1949. Bill J. Harley is on the other side."*

The Second Generation: Walter C. Davidson

Walter Davidson's second son, Walter C., joined Harley-Davidson and eventually became the vice-president of sales.

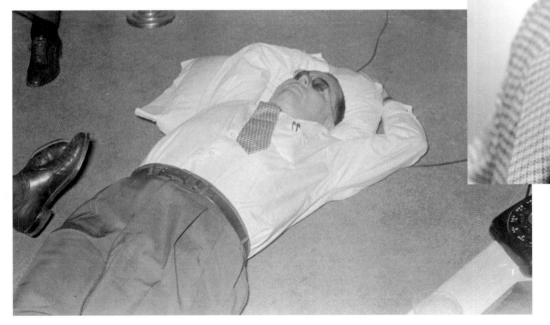

Jean Davidson: "Here's Walter hard at work during a sales trip to Texas in the 1950s. Someone wrote on the bottom of this photo, 'Please buy a motorcycle!'" (Katherine Davidson collection)

Above: *Jean Davidson: "Walter took over from Arthur Davidson in the sales department. He was a wild man in his day, but he took great care of his dealers and they loved him in return." (Katherine Davidson collection)*

Right: *Jean Davidson: "Here's Walter, left, in about 1929 when he was fifteen or sixteen, dressed in suit and tie for a spin on his motorcycle." (Katherine Davidson collection)*

The Second Generation: William James Harley

William Harley had two sons, William James and John Edward. They both soon joined the company, Bill as engineering vice-president. He stayed at Harley-Davidson until his death in 1971.

Mary Harley: "My father, Bill J. Harley, on his Big Twin. My dad rode to and from work every day, rain or shine, winter or summer. He often took me to school in a sidecar and picked me up in the afternoon. I remember him doing spins on his motorcycle for fun in front of the school to amuse the other kids." (Mary Harley Stocking collection)

May, 1957   21

HARLEY-DAVIDSON OFFICERS ADVANCED

DIRECTORS of the Harley-Davidson Motor Company advanced three officers in a recent meeting. William H. Davidson, president, announced the following changes in the company's top management:

William J. Harley was advanced to vice president, engineering; Walter C. Davidson advances to vice president, sales; and Otto P. Resech becomes the secretary and treasurer of the company.

Harley is a son of William S. Harley, one of the original founders of the company. A graduate in mechanical engineering at the University of Wisconsin, Harley joined the firm in 1934, became a director in 1937 and treasurer in 1943. He is a member of the Society of Automotive Engineers.

Davidson is also a son of an original founder, Walter Davidson. He joined the firm in 1936, became a director in 1943 and secretary in 1951.

Joining the firm as an accountant in 1934, Resech became assistant secretary in 1950 and a director in 1952. He is a member of the National Office Managers Association.

Gordon M. Davidson continues as vice president, manufacturing; and J. J. Balsom continues as the company's controller.

Spexarth Promoted to Chief Engineer

William J. Harley, vice president, engineering, has announced the promotion of Chris Spexarth to the position of chief engineer. Chris is an honor graduate of Marquette University, receiving his degree in mechanical engineering in 1931. He came directly to Harley-Davidson, became a designer in 1933, chief designer in 1937 and assistant engineer in 1943. He is also a member of the Society of Automotive Engineers.

Jean Davidson: "The promotion of Harley and Davidson family members were noted in The Enthusiast.*"*

Jean Davidson: "The first generation greets the second generation—both family members and motorcycles! Here was the introduction in 1948 of the Harley-Davidson two-stroke motorcycle, a short-lived attempt to enter the lightweight-motorcycle market. Presenting the new machine was, from left, Gordon Davidson, William J. Harley, Arthur Davidson, and William H. Davidson."

The Second Generation: John Edward Harley

William Harley's second son, John, joined Harley-Davidson and remained at the company until his death in 1976.

Jean Davidson: "On September 3, 1953, the founders' sons posed for this official portrait. From left: John Harley, product engineer; Walter C., secretary; William H., president; Gordon, vice-president; and William J. Harley, treasurer and chief engineer. Bill Davidson was fond of my grandfather, Walter, the company president. He shadowed Walter everywhere he went and became much like him in some respects. He didn't want to get his hands dirty down on the floor, preferring to run the company from his office. His son, William Godfrey, would become famous as Willie G. Davidson."

"Just like my grandfather, who was called the 'Silent Gray Fellow,' my dad was known as the 'Silver Fox' because his hair turned white when he was young, and he was completely gray by the time he was forty."
—Sarah Harley

Sarah Harley: "My father, John Harley, and my mother, Kathryn M. Harley, on the way to Daytona, Florida, in 1947. They met during a tank ride when my father was in the army at Fort Knox." (Sarah Harley-O'Hearn collection)

The Passing of the Founders

In 1950, Arthur Davidson passed away, the last of the original founders. The others had died in the late 1930s and early 1940s. Now the company was left to the next generation of Harleys and Davidsons to run.

NEWS BULLETIN

HARLEY-DAVIDSON MOTOR CO. • MILWAUKEE, WIS., U. S. A.

No. 1125   Jan. 15, 1951

ARTHUR DAVIDSON

FEBRUARY 11, 1881 ——— DECEMBER 30, 1950

Arthur Davidson
Secretary — General Sales Manager
HARLEY-DAVIDSON MOTOR COMPANY
FEBRUARY 11, 1881 — DECEMBER 30, 1950

THE entire community, countless friends everywhere, the world of motorcycling were shocked beyond words with the flashing of the news of the untimely death of Arthur Davidson and his beloved wife as the result of a tragic traffic accident. It seemed hard to believe that a man who did so much for his fellow men, who was so kind and generous, who helped pioneer the automotive age, who did so much for motorcycling, had been taken from us.

It was in the very early years of the present century that Arthur Davidson and his boyhood chum, William S. Harley, dreamed about taking the work out of pedaling a bicycle. Arthur Davidson was a pattern maker and William Harley was a draftsman. In their spare time, they labored and experimented, and in 1903 their first motorcycle took to the road. Soon they were joined in their efforts by Walter and William A. Davidson and thus emerged an association that for teamwork and effort was unique in the industry and led ultimately to the world-wide renown of the Harley-Davidson motorcycles.

As the new Harley-Davidson motorcycles gained favor and production increased, it devolved upon Arthur Davidson to take charge of sales. It was he who covered the country from coast to coast and established dealers. His ability to correctly size up situations and to judge men enabled him to make connections that produced volume sales for the growing Milwaukee plant.

Arthur Davidson's sound advice and counsel helped many a dealer over a rough spot. Dealers everywhere regarded him as their friend. It was he who appreciated the importance of competent mechanics to serve Harley-Davidson owners and the good work of the Harley-Davidson Service School is a tribute to his foresight. In the early days of advertising, he was quick to recognize this new force in selling, and he always insisted that the merits of Harley-Davidson products be kept constantly before the public. Noting the trend toward installment buying, the Kilbourn Finance Corporation was organized in 1923, and he was its president for many years.

Always interested in promoting the best aspects of motorcycling, Arthur Davidson naturally took an active interest in the American Motorcycle Association. For the last six years, he served as president and under his guidance many policies and programs were instituted to enlarge its scope and influence. Also, for the past six years, he was president of the Motorcycle and Allied Trades Association, an organization of members in the motorcycle industry.

To have met Arthur Davidson only once was always to remember him. His genial good humor, coupled with his fund of wholesome stories that invariably carried a subtle point he wanted to put over, added to his popularity. Never did he lose contact with his fellow men. To all, his door was always open and he was ready to listen, to give encouragement and advice.

Early in life, Arthur Davidson spent some time on a farm and the love of the soil remained with him. Some twenty years ago, he acquired 240 acres nine miles from the city. Here he built his home and developed a practical, paying farm, employing the most modern methods, stocked with pure-blooded Guernseys. There followed, of course, his great interest in the 4-H Club movement for the youth on the farm and his interest in the advancement of his favorite cattle. He was active in the American Guernsey Cattle Club, the Waukesha County Guernsey Breeders' Association and was a past president of the Milwaukee Farmers' Club.

(Continued on page 22)

Jean Davidson: "Founder William A. Davidson died in 1937, followed by Walter in 1942, William S. Harley in 1943, and Arthur in 1950. This was the special Harley-Davidson 'News Bulletin' sent out to all the dealers in tribute of Arthur's life."

"William S. Harley loved to golf—but he wasn't necessarily a good golfer. He'd enlist Arthur Davidson's son, Arthur Harley Davidson, as his caddie. If he got going on a hot round, he could stay out all evening playing until late at night. One time after dark during a good game, he made Arthur stand on the green in a white shirt and then aimed his drives at him."

—Sarah Harley

Sarah Harley: "William S. Harley died in 1943. He played a game of golf—one of his favorite pastimes—then walked into the clubhouse and died of a heart attack. He had sixty-seven engineering patents related to Harley-Davidson motorcycles at the time of his death." (Mary Harley Stocking collection)

Planning the Future From a Hospital Bed

The president of Harley-Davidson, Walter Davidson, died in 1942 at the age of sixty-six. Just before he died, Walter called his sons and nephews into his hospital room. He had made up his mind about who would take his place as the president of Harley-Davidson. Walter looked at the young men standing at his bedside and announced that William H. Davidson would take over his role of president. Gordon would be the vice-president of manufacturing. It was said that Walter Davidson was in charge right up to the end.

Right: *Jean Davidson: "This was the Harley-Davidson eulogy when Walter Davidson passed away on February 7, 1942."*

Far right: *Jean Davidson: "A clipping from a Milwaukee newspaper announcing my grandfather's passing."*

WALTER DAVIDSON
PRESIDENT

SEPTEMBER 30, 1876
FEBRUARY 7, 1942

WALTER DAVIDSON was a man of forceful personality, dynamic enthusiasm, keen judgment, and an executive who was representative of the highest ideals of American enterprise. These qualities, combined with his thorough knowledge of motorcycles and his interest in the sport of motorcycling, made him an outstanding figure in the industry and in the world of business. All who came in contact with him and those whose privilege it was to be associated with him deeply feel his loss.

Early in life, Walter Davidson learned the machinist trade. He worked in railroad shops here in Milwaukee and other cities. When Arthur Davidson and William S. Harley became interested in the designing of a motorcycle, it was but natural that Walter was consulted. Lending his spare time to the building of the first machine back in 1903, it was not long before the demand for additional motorcycles made it necessary for him to give up his work at the railroad shops and devote his full time to the growing motorcycle business. It was this business that held his principal interest to the end of his days and to which he unstintingly gave his best.

From building motorcycles to riding them was only one short step and soon Walter Davidson became one of the most enthusiastic competition riders. In 1908 he was awarded a diamond medal by the Federation of American Motorcyclists for his winning score made with a single cylinder Harley-Davidson in the greatest endurance run of that day. The course of this two-day classic started from Catskill, N. Y., and went to Brooklyn and around Long Island. Shortly thereafter, he established an economy record at Roslyn, Long Island, N. Y., covering fifty miles of hilly road on one quart and one ounce of gasoline. His competition achievements did much to bring Harley-Davidson motorcycles national recognition. A case filled with beautiful trophies attests to his many victories on hill, road and track.

Being both a full-fledged machinist and a competition rider, it naturally followed that Walter Davidson insisted on the highest quality

PRESIDENT OF MOTORCYCLE FIRM IS DEAD

Walter Davidson, 65, Dies in Hospital Saturday

Walter Davidson, 65, whose name has been synonymous with the manufacture of motorcycles for almost 40 years, died Saturday at Milwaukee hospital where he had been confined since an operation several weeks ago. He lived at 3816 N. Lake dr.

Funeral services will be held Tuesday at 2 p. m. at the Philip Weiss chapel, 1901 N. Farwell av. Burial will be in Forest Home cemetery.

As president and general manager of the Harley-Davidson Motor co. he was actively in charge of the business until he was taken ill. With his brothers, Arthur and William A., and William Harley, he founded the firm in 1903 in a small shack at N. Thirty-seventh st. and W. Juneau av. From this small beginning, the company prospered and grew until today it occupies several square blocks on the same site.

STARTED IN RAIL SHOP

Born in Milwaukee, Mr. Davidson as a youth started work in the railroad shops here to learn the machinist's trade. After a few years, he quit that job and with his brothers and young Bill Harley, started to turn out a crude motorcycle in the small shanty.

As the men developed and improved their first product, the company expanded to take its place as the leading motorcycle manufacturing concern in the world, with a machine rolling off the assembly line every five minutes.

Its constantly increasing business was stimulated by the great military demand for motorcycles which took the Harley-Davidson machine into all corners of the globe.

WALTER DAVIDSON

Jean Davidson: "After Walter's death, my grandmother Emma Davidson kept on traveling in style with all of her lady friends in the 1950s. Here she is at far right on a camel in Egypt. She was a gutsy lady." (Katherine Davidson collection)

Jean Davidson: "My father followed William Davidson, as the works manager. He was happiest being down on the floor of the factory overseeing the machine tools and talking with the workers. My father was completely involved in the building of the motorcycles, so much so that he would forget to change and wore the same clothes to work for three days in a row. Here he was in 1965 when he was the vice-president of manufacturing."

Harley-Davidson at War

When the United States entered World War I in 1917, the U.S. Army took a cavalry mounted on Harley-Davidsons to Europe. In the next two years, the army bought about 20,000 motorcycles for dispatch work and as scout vehicles.

In World War II, Harley-Davidson supplied its WLC and WLA motorcycles to the military and also built numerous other items for the armed services.

Right: *Jean Davidson: "The Harley-Davidson shaft-drive XA. As old-time dealer Hap Jameson remembered: 'It cost the company a fortune and wasn't worth a penny.'*

Facing page: *Sarah Harley: "My father, John Harley, was a captain in the U.S. Army. He was in charge of teaching the soldiers how to drive and maintain motorcycles. Here he is at Fort Knox, Kentucky, in the early 1940s." (Sarah Harley-O'Hearn collection)*

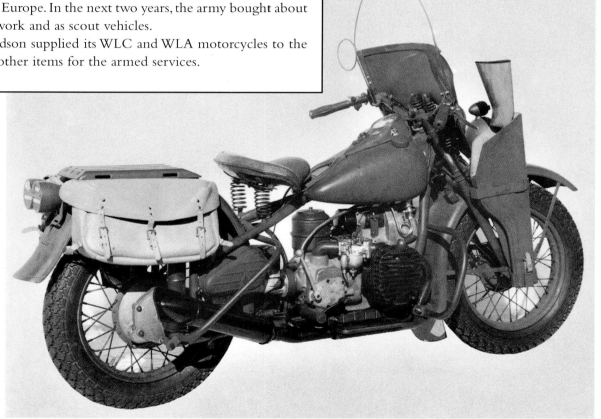

Facing page: *Sarah Harley: "My father also taught police officers to ride their Harley-Davidsons. Here he is in 1945 with the evening shift motorcycle patrolmen of the Birmingham, Alabama, Police Department."* (Sarah Harley-O'Hearn collection)

Left: *Sarah Harley: "Here is grandfather William S. Harley, center, and my father, John, right, at Fort Knox during a visit. Eventually, Harley-Davidson needed my dad back at the factory to help run things, so they petitioned the army to release him, which they did in 1943 or 1944."* (Sarah Harley-O'Hearn collection)

Celebrating Fifty Years of Motorcycles

Facing page: *Jean Davidson: "Here is the official photograph from the fiftieth anniversary dinner. Standing at right are my mom and dad, Doris and Gordon. Next to them are Bill and Ann Harley. Seated at left is Walter and Betty Davidson. Seated at the far right are Bill and Ruth Davidson, Willie G.'s parents."*

In 1953, Harley-Davidson celebrated its first fifty years of building motorcycles. Ironically—and sadly—Harley-Davidson's arch-rival Indian was at the same time struggling for its livelihood and would shortly go out of business.

Behind the scenes, the founders at Harley and Indian had long been friends. Arthur Davidson raised one of the finest herds of Guernsey cows in Wisconsin. George Hendee, one of the founders of the Indian "motocycle," also raised prize Guernseys. Because of their bovine hobbies and in spite of their motorcycle "day jobs," Arthur and George became close friends and spent hours comparing their cattle businesses—as well as their motorcycle businesses. Thus, the demise of Indian in 1953 was seen as a sad affair at Harley-Davidson.

Jean Davidson: "By the time the cake was cut to celebrate Harley-Davidson's fiftieth anniversary, the sons were running the firm. From left, here's William H., Walter C., Gordon, and Bill J. Harley."

Growing Up Harley-Davidson

The founders' sons and daughters in turn had numerous children, many of whom grew up together in Milwaukee or at their families' lake homes in the summertime.

Right: *Jean Davidson: "Here I am in my grand-aunt Clara's lap with Grandpa Walter holding my elder sister, Barbara, in 1938."*

Facing page: *Jean Davidson: "Motorcycles, big deal! I wanted a horse! Motorcycles were everywhere in my life as a child, so I never thought much about them. The grass is always greener on the other side of the fence: I wanted that horse and felt I was a deprived child!"*

"I remember in 1970 meeting Soichiro Honda, the founder of the Honda motorcycle and car company. He came out to our house on Beaver Lake in Hartland, Wisconsin, to talk with my dad, John Harley, about AMA or Motorcycle Industry Council business. I was just a young girl, and I said to Mr. Honda, 'You're so little. Is that why you make little motorcycles?' Well, my dad immediately shushed me, but Mr. Honda didn't seem to care. He invited us to what he called his 'ranch' in Japan to ride horses with his two sons. Unfortunately, we never went."

—Sarah Harley

Jean Davidson: "My children all grew up riding motorcycles—although we started them off on small machines, not Harley-Davidsons."

Right: Sarah Harley: "I first rode on a motorcycle when I was just a couple days old. My dad drove and my mom carried me. There are no pictures of us as children on motorcycles. They were just everyday transportation, never anything special to us. I preferred sailing. My love of motorcycles came later: Here I am in 1994 with my friend Mike Monday on top of some mountain in Colorado." (Sarah Harley-O'Hearn collection)

Jean Davidson: "Here's my daughter Sue in the sidecar after getting married to Steve Lee. The ride of choice was again a Knucklehead."

Jean Davidson: "This is my son Bill and his new wife, Tique, riding a 1940 Knucklehead after their wedding. The motorcycle started on fire when two wires shorted out in the battery compartment as they arrived at the reception, but Bill managed to stomp out the flames."

Sarah Harley: "On our way to Sturgis in 1994, my friend Mike Monday and I rode 5,000 miles in ten days. Here we are at the entrance to Badlands National Park." (Sarah Harley-O'Hearn collection)

Jean Davidson: "Here's my son Jon taking friends for a spin on our Harley-Davidson snowmobile. The snowmobiles ran like champs, but they were so heavy that if you got stuck, you were really stuck."

Racing Head to Head With Indian

By the 1940s, racing primarily meant one thing to Harley-Davidson: doing battle with the archrival Indian firm. There was some competition from English makers such as Norton, but the true battle was between the two surviving American motorcycle makers for the checkered flag on Sunday and cycle sales on Monday.

Facing page: *Jean Davidson: "Once Harley-Davidson started racing, the company went at it full steam. Here's the start of a race in the 1940s."*

Above: *Jean Davidson: "This photo was taken at an AMA Competition Committee meeting in Daytona Beach, Florida, in 1942. These were the powers that be who set the rules for American motorcycle racing—and also built and sold the motorcycles. Talk about a conflict of interest! Seated are Bill J. Harley on the far right, Walter third from right, Arthur center, and John Harley second from the left. Now that's a stacked deck." (Robert Jameson collection)*

Above: *Jean Davidson: "I looked forward to going to the motorcycle races at the Wisconsin State Fair Park each year. To me, the sound of revving engines was pure exhilaration. My mother and sister did not like the dirt and the noise. I couldn't get enough of it."*

Right: *Jean Davidson: "My dad knew all the racers, so he would take me into the pits while he talked and joked with them. Through the years, many of the champion racers came to our home. Brad Andres, who won the national championship in 1954, would stop by."*

Jean Davidson: "Naturally I wondered why there weren't any tomboys in the world of motorcycle racing. To me, this was just another example of how girls never had as much fun as boys."

Left: *Jean Davidson: "Happy times for Harley-Davidson after factory rider Ben Campanale won the 1938 Daytona Beach 200. William S. Harley shakes his hand on the left while Walter C. Davidson stands at right."*

Above: *Jean Davidson: "I dreamed of racing, but in those days a girl would not have been allowed on the racetrack except to kiss the winner and hand him his trophy. The kissing was fine by me, but it was the racing that I wished for. The racers were usually rough around the edges, which made them all the more exciting to a young teenage girl. My dad would listen to the stories of life in the racing world, and I would sit there entranced by their tales. I was always in awe of their light-hearted manner when it came to the dangers of racing and the injuries they sustained in the course of a year."*

My Friend
"Jean Davidson"
Carroll Resweber #1

Carroll Resweber

Jean Davidson: "Carroll Resweber was one of Harley-Davidson's top riders in the 1950s. Carroll was also a good friend of my uncle, Walter C. Davidson, who took care of all of the racing expenses. When Carroll was seriously injured in a race, the hospital said they would have to amputate his foot. Walter said, 'No way!' and had Carroll flown to a Milwaukee hospital on his bill. Here, they were able to save his foot."

The Motorcycle of the Stars

It wasn't until the 1950s that Harley-Davidsons truly started becoming an American icon. Over time, movie, television, and music stars began riding Harley-Davidsons for fun, which in turn helped make the motorcycles appear stylish. The glitter rubbed off on Harley-Davidson, and soon the motorcycles were stars themselves.

Jean Davidson: "Gone With the Wind star Clark Gable was ahead of his time in riding a Harley-Davidson. Here he is on a Big Twin in 1942."

Singing cowboy Roy Rogers on a Big Twin in 1958.

Jean Davidson: "I remember watching Elvis on television in the 1950s. My dad, Gordon, came into the room, shook his head, and laughed, 'That young man sure can swivel his hips!' But as soon as his first records went gold, Elvis bought a Harley-Davidson, which he rode as if it were a throne. From then on, he purchased a new Harley-Davidson every year. My uncle Walter used to have to run all around the factory to find Elvis exactly the motorcycle that he wanted."

Good and Bad Reputations

A motorcycle race and the following celebration in the sleepy little town of Hollister, California, on July 4, 1947, changed the public's attitude toward motorcycles forever. Motorcycle clubs like the Hell's Angels, the Outlaws, Satan's Pals, the Boozefighters, and many others started up, and motorcycling suddenly got stuck with a bad reputation in the mid 1950s. This image tarnished Harley-Davidson as well, and the company spent decades fighting to regain its earlier sterling reputation.

Jean Davidson: "Motorcycles had mostly a good reputation up into the 1950s. Here was a typical Harley-Davidson publicity photo from about 1951 showing two youngsters out enjoying the sun on their Panhead."

Jean Davidson: "The bad boy look was becoming the rage with motorcycle riders in the 1950s. My cousin Willie G. rode a Harley-Davidson but he was about as clean-cut as they came. Here's Willie G. and his brother John in 1952. Most of my male cousins rode motorcycles, simply because their fathers did. Other kids had cars, but we got motorcycles."

Left: *Jean Davidson: "Now suddenly motorcycles had a bad reputation, and this tarnished Harley-Davidson's corporate image as well. President Bill Davidson fought tooth and nail for decades to retain Harley-Davidson's image with advertising photos like this from 1964."*

Below: *Jean Davidson: "Harley-Davidson had always had a good reputation from its founding. Harley-Davidsons always led the victory parades after World War II and any other parades that took place in Milwaukee, especially the Fourth of July celebrations. Harley-Davidson motorcycles were viewed as being as American as apple pie."*

"I remember my dad, John Harley, sitting around the dinner table and talking about starting HOG—the Harley-Davidson Owners Group—way back in 1973. They were concerned that they didn't want Harley-Davidson riders to be seen as just a big, bad motorcycle gang, but as good people."
—Sarah Harley

Jean Davidson: "I saw The Wild One and several of the other motorcycle movies of the time and of course was attracted to the wild side of the rider too. I sympathized with the Marlon Brando character: All he wanted was to be understood. Just like me."

Jean Davidson: "The Wild One *came out in 1953, and motorcycle gangs suddenly were a big deal. The film began with a warning that was designed to scare the public—and did: 'This is a shocking story. It could never take place in most American towns—but it did in this one. It is a public challenge not to let it happen again.'"*

Left: *Jean Davidson: "Marlon Brando didn't ride a Harley in* The Wild One—*he rode a Triumph Thunderbird—but the movie's true bad guy, Lee Marvin as Chino, did. Suddenly, Harley-Davidsons—and all motorcycles—were viewed by the public as bad, and all motorcyclists were branded as 'outsiders.'"*

Above: *Jean Davidson: "Willie G. and I went together to see* Easy Rider *when it first came out in 1969. I remember crying over that sad, tragic ending. I wanted it to be happy and didn't understand why people were so strongly against motorcyclists at the time."*

Other Ventures and Other Venues

Through the years, Harley-Davidson attempted to diversify into other products, from bicycles to golf carts. None of these ever panned out for the company, and through it all, motorcycles remained the heart and soul of Harley-Davidson.

Jean Davidson: "Walter C. Davidson was a big advocate of the golf cart venture—he firmly believed in it. The photo they're showing off was taken at the Bluemound Country Club in Wauwatosa, where he was a member. Sadly, the golf carts never really worked out due to emission controls on its gas engine, which priced the golf cart right out of the market. Still, Arthur Harley Davidson and Johnny Harley had great fun testing the carts at a Milwaukee golf course, as they were both avid golfers."

"I remember my dad gave my brother Pat a Harley-Davidson Sprint for Christmas one year. It was in a crate beside the Christmas tree. They moved it down into the basement to put it together, but they couldn't get the kickstand on. My dad was pounding on it with a hammer, getting angrier and angrier. Finally, he called the factory and someone came to pick it up. They used a big old hammer—whack!—and got the kickstand in. For years after that, the joke around the factory was that you had to use a bigger hammer to get things done."
—Sarah Harley

Above: *Jean Davidson: "Walter Davidson is sitting here on one of the two-stroke motorcycles Harley-Davidson made in the 1950s. These were good little machines, but just didn't fit the company's image and were soon dropped."*

Right: *Jean Davidson: "Harley-Davidson's motorscooter, the Topper, was an effort to cash in on the popularity of the scooters from Cushman and the Vespa and Lambretta from Italy, which were all sold through Sears, Roebuck and Montgomery Ward stores. Unfortunately, the Topper didn't really top them all, as this ad had promised."*

New! A Scooter by
HARLEY-DAVIDSON

Tops them all in beauty and performance
...it's the TOPPER

Fun-loving Jacks (and Jills, too) are jumping at the
chance to meet the new Harley-Davidson Topper.
And why not? There's not another motor scooter like
it — combining clean, smart beauty with the newest
mechanical secrets of success. Scootaway automatic
transmission makes riding a snap . . . lowest center of
gravity makes handling a dream. See the new
Topper at your Harley-Davidson dealer.
Or write for free, colorful folder.

HARLEY-DAVIDSON MOTOR CO.
Milwaukee 1, Wisconsin, Dept. P
World's leading manufacturer of lightweight motor vehicles

Evel Knievel, All-American Motorcycling Hero

In the 1960s and early 1970s, Evel Knievel became an all-American hero like no other. Harley-Davidson provided Evel with his All-American Motorcycle, an XR-750. Harley-Davidson was sponsoring Evel to promote—perhaps ironically—a better image for motorcycling.

Jean Davidson: "For his show in Chicago, we sat in the front row and watched intently as he warmed up his Harley-Davidson. It was very exciting, and we all crossed our fingers that he didn't get hurt or killed. The crowd yelled and cheered until finally Evel made his final approach. His jump went just as planned except they had to open the doors at the end of the auditorium because he was going so fast there was not enough room for him to stop. I took this snapshot of him in midair."

Jean Davidson: "Here I am in front of Evel Knievel's truck before the Chicago show with Nancy, Willie G.'s wife, and all our children."

Jean Davidson: "In 1971, Willie G. and I were invited with our families to be special guests of Evel Knievel when he came to Chicago to put on his death-defying show for the public. On the way there, I told the children that anyone who would do such crazy stunts as jumping a motorcycle over nineteen cars must not be very smart. Much to my surprise, Evel was gracious and friendly. I found him to be an interesting person. When I talked to him before the show, he seemed perfectly calm and logical—even though he made his living jumping motorcycles."

The Sale and Buy-Back of Harley-Davidson

In the mid 1960s, several Harley and Davidson family members wanted to diversify some of their assets. So, in 1965, Harley-Davidson went public. To fight off a takeover attempt by the Bangor Punta Corporation, the Harley-Davidson board of directors went in search of a friendly buyer for the company. In late 1968, the directors recommended selling to American Machine and Foundry (AMF). The sale took place in January 1969, and Bill Davidson stayed on as president under the direction of AMF and its chairman, Rodney C. Gott.

On February 26, 1981, a group of Harley-Davidson executives signed a letter of intent with AMF to purchase the company. On June 16, 1981, the deal was finally completed. Harley-Davidson was again a private company, and Willie G. was one of the owners along with AMF's Vaughn Beals, Harley-Davidson President Charles Thompson, and several others.

Jean Davidson: "This was the first Harley-Davidson board meeting following my father's death earlier in 1967."

"I remember going to the stockholder meetings and listening to the arguments for and against the sale. There was a lot of yelling and much sadness. I remember thinking that I was glad that my father did not live to see this; he would have been sick at the thought of selling. The family members had little choice because they were in trouble: They had all their money invested in the company and needed capital for their own companies, projects, and to live. And Harley-Davidson was in trouble largely due to the arrival of the Japanese motorcycle makers. The families of the founders were torn apart by their strong feelings, but in the end they knew what had to be done: They had to sell."

—Jean Davidson

Jean Davidson: "In 1959, at the ripe old age of twenty-one, I got married to John Oeflein. In 1968, we bought the Harley-Davidson franchise for Milwaukee County—the Knuth brothers' old franchise—and built a new store at 6312 West Fond du Lac Avenue while retaining the south-side store at 1753 South Muskeego Avenue. We named our company Milwaukee Harley-Davidson, Inc. and became the largest dealer in Wisconsin."

Celebrating 100 Years of the Harley-Davidson Family

Jean Davidson: "A gathering of Davidsons at the September 2001 Milwaukee Home Run rally. From left, that's Willie G.; Kathy Davidson Bruce; my eldest daughter, Lori Jean Davidson Walker; myself; Willie G's wife, Nancy; and Karen Davidson of MotorClothes fame."

As Harley-Davidson celebrated its centennial, the year also marked a celebration of the legacy of the Harley and Davidson families. The first Harleys and Davidsons had come to the United States from England and Scotland almost 150 years earlier, and their great-grandchildren were now honoring the families' motorcycling tradition.

Jean Davidson: "Here I am with my great-uncle, Arthur Harley Davidson. The son of founder Arthur Davidson, his middle name was in honor of Arthur's best friend, William S. Harley."

Jean Davidson: "Here is my grandson, Nicolas Davidson Oeflein, the fifth generation of Davidsons to wear the original Scottish suit first worn by the founders' sons."

"Willie G. has developed his talents to the fullest, and I am glad that he is representing the Davidson legacy at Harley-Davidson. He reinforces my strong-held belief: Find your unique gifts, develop them, and then use them to serve yourself and your community. It is a tribute to all that I believe in when someone like Willie G. has stayed with our grandfathers' dream of working to make the Harley-Davidson motorcycle the best it can be."

—Jean Davidson

Sarah Harley: "Here's Willie G. and me sharing fashion tips at the Rapid City Convention Center in 1994." (Sarah Harley-O'Hearn collection)

Sarah Harley: "Harley-Davidson's ninetieth: From left, my cousin Roseanne Harley-Wright, brother James Patrick Harley, and me." (Sarah Harley-O'Hearn collection)

Above: *Sarah Harley: "Here's the Harley family on our motorcycles in 1998. From left, Pat Harley; John E. Harley Jr. with his wife, Kate, and their 95th Anniversary Road Glide; Bruce O-Hearn and me on my 95th Anniversary Springer Heritage Softail; William Harley on his XLCR; and Jessica M. Harley on a classic." (Sarah Harley-O'Hearn collection)*

Right: *Sarah Harley: "This is my brother, James Patrick Harley. Injured in a motorcycle accident when he was younger, it has not stopped him from riding, as you can see here." (Sarah Harley-O'Hearn collection)*

Sarah Harley: "Here I am in the center celebrating Harley-Davidson's ninetieth anniversary in Milwaukee in 1993 with ZZ Top—from left, Frank Beard, Dusty Hill, and, far right, Billy Gibbons—as well as Miss Harley-Davidson, Gina Galligan." (Sarah Harley-O'Hearn collection)

Above: *Jean Davidson: "The next generation of Harleys and Davidsons! The launch party for my book* Growing Up Harley-Davidson *brought together many members of the Harley and Davidson family. Here is Natalie, great-great-granddaughter of Arthur Davidson, right, and Madeline, the great-great-granddaughter of William S. Harley."*

Right: *Jean Davidson: "Here I am in 2001 just before the publication of my first book,* Growing Up Harley-Davidson.*"*